100 Games to Play

Written by Rebecca Gilpin
Designed by Catherine Mackinnon
Illustrated by Antonia Miller

Contents

Follow the leader

This game's really funny if lots of people are playing. Before you start, choose someone to be the leader.

1 Everyone stands in a line behind the leader.
They have to copy what she does, such as:

Leader

Hopping...

waving their arms...

or jumping...

2 Anyone who doesn't copy an action correctly is out. The last person still playing is the next leader.

Guess the tune

1 Someone thinks of a tune for the others to guess.

2 They hum the first line of the tune, and the others try to guess what it is. Each person has one guess:

hmm, hmm, hmm, hmmmm...

Ooh, is it...?

3 If someone guesses correctly, it's their turn to think of a new tune. If not, the first person hums the first two lines from their tune:

hmm, hmm, hmm, hmmmm... hmm, hmm, hmm, hmm-hmm...

4 The game continues with a line being added each time, and the others trying to guess what the tune is.

5 If no one's guessed after a whole verse or by the end of the tune, the humming person says what it is.

Kick the can

Play this in a big space. Draw around an empty can on the ground with a chalk, and choose someone to be 'it'.

1 Everyone runs off to hide while 'it' stands next to the can and counts to 50, with her eyes shut.

6...7...8...

2 When she gets to 50, she shouts Here I come!, then tries to find the hiders. This is what happens next:

The hiders try to get to the can and kick it before 'it' spots them. If a hider does this, he is safe and hides again while 'it' puts the can back in the circle...

If 'it' spots a hider, she races him to the can. If she gets there first, she kicks the can and shouts his name. He is caught, and has to put the can back and stand next to it...

...until another hider kicks the can and rescues him (and anyone else who has been caught). The rescuer replaces the can and they run off.

3 The game ends when 'it' has caught everyone at the same time. The last one to be caught is the next 'it'.

Group story

In this game, everyone contributes to a story, one sentence at a time. Try to make each sentence easy to follow with another one.

1 Someone starts by making up a sentence. It can be long or short.

> As she crunched through the snow, Leila looked up and saw a tall stone tower...

> In the darkness, she could see light glowing around the edges of a door...

2 Someone else adds another sentence.

3 Everyone takes turns adding a new sentence:

> She crept up to the tower and tried the door handle.

> The door scraped open with a loud 'Creeeak'.

> Leila tiptoed inside.

4 The person who ends the story starts a new one.

Scuttling crab race

Play this game on a sandy beach.

1 Draw two lines in the sand, about 20 paces apart.

Start

Finish

2 Everyone stands at the start and bends over, next to the line, like this. Then, someone shouts:

Ready... GO!

Everyone puts their hands and feet on the ground.

3 Everyone scuttles sideways like a crab. The first to get to the finish line wins.

Finish

Variations
• Backwards: try a backwards running race, but look over your shoulder, so that you don't fall over!
• Hopping: race on one leg.

Squiggle drawings

To play this game, you'll need some paper and pens and pencils. You could also play this on a beach by drawing in the sand.

1 One person draws a squiggle with a pen or pencil.

This squiggle could become...

2 The other person uses a different pen or pencil to turn the squiggle into a drawing.

a bird...   or a fish.

3 Take turns drawing a squiggle on the paper, then turning it into a drawing of something.

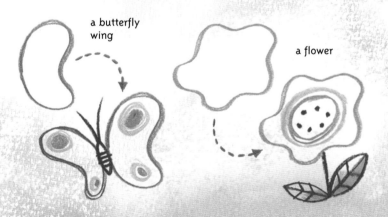

a butterfly wing

a flower

Ice Monster

For this game, you need to be near a wall.
Choose someone to be the Ice Monster.

1️⃣ The Ice Monster stands facing the wall,
with his back to everyone else...

Ice Monster

Keep an eye
on the Ice
Monster.

He shouts Go! and everyone else
runs around behind him.

2️⃣ Suddenly, the Ice Monster turns
around and shouts:

FREEZE!

3️⃣ Everyone else stops running and
stands totally still, as if they're frozen.

4️⃣ If the Ice Monster sees anyone move, they're out. Everyone
has to stay still until he shouts Go! again.

5️⃣ The Ice Monster faces the wall again, and the game continues.
The last person still playing wins the game.

Spotting picture

For this game, you'll need paper, pens and pencils.

1 Take turns spotting between six and ten things around you and writing them in a list.

a hairy dog

a red umbrella

a fluffy cloud

a blue hat

a bunch of roses

a dark-haired girl

2 Then, each person draws a picture that includes everything on the list.

3 Have fun mixing everything up. Here are some pictures made from the list above:

Variation
If you are alone, make the list yourself.

Chasing shadows

Play this game in a big space on a bright sunny day.

1 Choose someone to be 'it'.

'It'

2 Everyone else runs around and 'it' tries to 'tag' (touch) them by stepping on their shadows.

3 If someone is tagged, they are out...

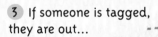

...and they stand out of the way while the game continues.

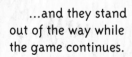

4 The game ends when 'it' has tagged everyone. In the next game, the first person who was tagged is 'it'.

Squish-squash

1 In this counting game, some numbers are replaced with squish, squash and squish-squash.
You'll need to know your 3 and 5 times tables.

 Squish
Numbers that can be divided by 3, such as: 3, 6, 9, 12, 15, 18, and so on.

 Squash
Numbers that can be divided by 5, such as: 5, 10, 20, 25, 35, 40, and so on.

Squish-squash
Numbers that can be divided by both 3 and 5, such as: 15 or 30.

2 Count up from 1, taking turns to say a number:

1...   2...   3...   4...   5...   6...

One   Two   Squish   Four   Squash   Squish

3 Continue for as long as you can. If anyone hesitates or makes a mistake, they're out:

27...   28...   29...   30...   31...

Squish!   Twenty-eight   Twenty-nine   Squish-squash   Um... er...

Funny faces chain

To play this game, everyone has to be able to see each other's faces.

1 Someone makes a face, such as:

A big 'O' mouth...

2 The next person makes the same face, then adds a new face of their own:

They make a
big 'O' mouth...

...then blink
their eyes twice.

3 Everyone takes turns adding a new face, making all the faces in the correct order:

Big 'O' mouth   Blinking eyes   Sad face

4 If someone makes the faces in the wrong order or forgets a face, they're out.

Word catch

To play this game, you need a ball.

1 One person thinks of a five-letter word to play the game with.

WATER

2 Both people take turns throwing the ball to each other.

3 If someone drops or misses the ball, they get the first letter of the word:

W . . . .

4 Each time someone drops or misses the ball, they get another letter.

WAT . .   W . . . .

5 If anyone gets all the letters in the word, they're out.

No yes, no no

1 One person asks someone else a question that they would usually answer Yes or No:

> Are you hungry?

> I am, actually.

2 The other person has to answer without saying Yes or No, or nodding or shaking their head.

3 The first person asks another question, and the second person answers without saying Yes or No.

> Is the sun shining?

> I believe it is.

4 The game continues until the second person makes a mistake and says Yes or No, or nods or shakes their head. Then it's their turn to ask questions.

Hot and cold

Find a small object to play the game with, such as a coin or a stone, then choose someone to be the seeker.

1 The seeker leaves the room and someone else hides the object.

2 The seeker comes back in, and has to try to find the object. He moves slowly around the room.

3 Everyone calls out to help him to find the object. If he moves away from it, he gets 'colder', and if he moves closer to it, he gets 'warmer':

Moving away from the object...

Cold!

Very cold!

FREEZING!

Moving closer to the object...

Warm!

Hotter!

BOILING!

4 Continue calling out until the seeker finds the object.

Monster doodles

Each person needs some paper and pens, or you could play it by drawing in the sand on a beach.

1 Each person draws a shape for a monster's body, then passes their paper to someone else.

2 Someone tells everyone what to draw next...

Draw eyes...

...and everyone adds that part of the monster.

3 Everyone passes on their piece of paper, then someone else tells everyone what to draw next.

4 Continue the game with everyone adding to the monsters each time they're passed on:

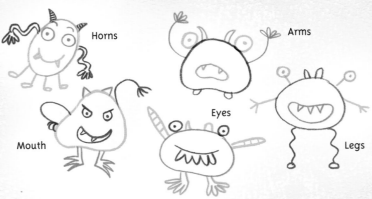

Horns

Arms

Eyes

Mouth

Legs

Endless questions

In this game, two people talk to each other and can only ask questions. Ask someone else to be a referee.

1 One person starts by asking a question:

Why do ducks quack?

Do you think they should bark instead?

2 The other person replies with a question that follows on logically from the first one, as quickly as they can.

3 They take turns, and the referee listens closely. If anyone hesitates for too long or gives an answer that isn't a question, the referee tells them that they're out.

Shouldn't barking be left to dogs?

...um... er...um...

Sorry, you're out!

No one can argue with the referee.

4 Whoever is out first is the referee in the next game.

23

Shark tag

Play this game on a sandy beach. Draw two wavy
lines in the sand for coral reefs, about 20 paces apart.

1 One person is a shark, and everyone else is a fish. The shark
stands in the ocean, and the fish run from reef to reef. The shark
tries to 'tag' (touch) the fish, but can only do this when they're
in the ocean.

2 When the shark tags a fish, that fish becomes another shark.
Both sharks then chase the other fish.

3 Continue the game until there are no fish left.

Memory game

To play this game, you'll need some objects, a cloth, some paper and pens or pencils.

1 One person goes into a room and everyone else waits outside. He puts several objects on the floor...

...then completely covers them with a cloth.

2 He lets the others in, then uncovers the objects. He gives everyone two minutes to try to remember what is there, then he covers the objects again.

3 Everyone writes down as many objects as they can remember. Whoever remembers the most wins.

Where do I live?

1 Someone thinks of a place (not where they really live) for everyone else to try to guess. It could be:

a country...   a place...   a building...

Italy

2 Everyone else tries to guess the place, taking turns asking questions that can be answered Yes or No. They have 20 questions altogether.

Is it made from bricks?

Is it a country?

No... Yes!

It's Italy!

3 If someone thinks they know what the place is, they can guess. If they are correct, they win. If not, the guess counts as one of the 20 questions.

4 If no one manages to guess the place, the person who thought of it has won.

Hopscotch

Hopscotch is a hopping game, played with a pebble. If you step on a line at any time, you have to start again. If two or more people are playing, they take turns.

The grid

1. Draw the grid on the ground with a chalk, then play the game:

Throw the pebble onto square 1. Hop over square 1, and land on 2 on one foot...

Hop again and land with one foot on square 3 and one on 4...

Hop onto 5, 6 and 7, then hop onto 8. Jump around, then hop back to 2. Pick up the pebble...

...hop onto 1, then hop off the end of the grid.

If you make a mistake or put your other foot down, you have to start again.

2. Continue in the same way, throwing the pebble onto 2, then onto 3, then onto 4, and so on. Always hop over the square that the pebble is in.

3. Play until you have picked up the pebble from each of the squares on the grid.

Musical statues

For this game, you need something that plays music. Choose someone to be the referee, who will also be in charge of the music.

1 The referee starts the music...

...and everyone else dances or moves around the room.

2 Suddenly, the referee stops the music and everyone else has to stand totally still, like a statue.

Breathing movements are allowed.

3 The referee looks to see if anyone is moving. The first person he sees moving is out.

4 The referee starts the music and everyone starts to move again.

5 The game continues until only one person is still playing. They become the referee in the next game.

I spy

1 Someone looks for an object that everyone can see, but they don't tell the others what it is.

> I spy with my little eye, something beginning with S...

2 They say I spy with my little eye, something beginning with... followed by the first letter of the object.

> Street?

> Sky?

3 Everyone else takes turns guessing things that they can see that start with that letter.

4 The first person to guess correctly looks for a new object for everyone else to guess.

Variation
Give a word clue instead of a letter, such as: I spy with my little eye, something blue...

Line of four

This game is played using a piece of paper and a pen.

1 Start by drawing seven lines across the paper, and seven lines down it, to make a grid:

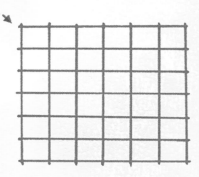

2 Take turns writing your initial in a square.

 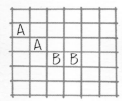 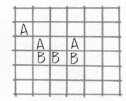

3 The winner is the first person to write their initial in a line of four squares.

Here are some of the ways to make a line of four:

 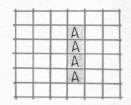

One behind

The faster you play this game, the funnier it is.

1 Everyone sits or stands in a circle, and someone silently pretends to do an action, such as singing:

2 Whoever is next to them asks:

> What are you doing?

3 ...and they say something different from the action that they're actually doing.

> I'm brushing my hair.

4 The second person pretends to do what's just been said...

> I'm brushing my teeth.

5 ...and the next person asks what she's doing. She says any action other than the one that she's doing.

> I'm riding a horse.

6 That person then does the action that she's said, and the game continues. If anyone does the wrong action, they're out.

Piggy in the middle

You can play this game with any kind of ball.

1 Choose someone to be the piggy. The piggy stands in the middle of everyone else.

Piggy

2 Throw the ball back and forth, trying not to let the piggy catch it.

Piggy

3 If the piggy catches the ball, she changes places with the person who threw it.

4 Continue to play until everyone has been the piggy.

New piggy

Variation
Bounce the ball to each other instead of throwing it.

Spotting game

Play this game in a busy place, such as a train station or an airport. You'll need paper and pens or pencils.

1 Each person writes down three things that they might be able to spot where they are, such as:

2 They each add the things to their list:

3 One person says *Go!* and everyone tries to spot the things on the list. If someone spots something, they shout *Spotted!*, point at it, and win a point. Everyone else crosses it off their list.

4 When everything has been spotted, add up everyone's points. Whoever has the most points wins.

Word finder

Each person needs a piece of paper and a pen.
The goal is to find words hidden inside a long word.

1 Someone thinks of a long word, and
everyone writes it down.

daydreaming

2 Everyone has five minutes to
write down as many words as they
can, using only the letters in the
long word:

and ✔ an ✗   dreamy ✔ dreamer ✗

All words have to be at least
three letters long.

Only use each letter once in a word, unless
it appears more than once.

The word 'daydreaming' contains these words...

dreamy   red   dame   gem   danger   mad game   rainy   adder   grand   drama

...and many more.

3 After three minutes, everyone checks that they
are happy that each other's words are real words.

4 Then, add up the scores.
Whoever has the most points is
the winner.

Three-letter words: 3 points
Four-letter words: 4 points
...and so on.

Hide-and-seek

Agree the boundaries of where you're going to play. Choose somewhere as a base, and choose a seeker.

1 The seeker stands at the base and counts to 30, with his eyes shut. Everyone else runs off to hide.

24...25...26...

Base

2 When the seeker has finished counting, he shouts Here I come, ready or not! and looks for the hiders.

If he spots a hider in a hiding place, they're out...

I see you!

...but a hider can leave their hiding place to run to the base. If they get there, they're safe.

If the seeker sees someone running to the base, he tries to get there first. If he reaches the base before the hider does, the hider is out.

3 The last person still hiding is the winner. The hider who was found first is the seeker in the next game.

Ship to shore

In this game, everyone has to do what the captain says.

1 Draw a line in the sand on a beach or on the ground with a chalk. Then, choose a captain.

2 The captain stands at the end of the line and everyone else stands with a foot on each side of it.

Ship

Shore

Captain

One side of the line is a ship and the other is the shore.

3 The captain shouts Ship! or Shore! at random. Everyone has to jump to that side of the line.

Sh......ip!

Ship

Shore

The captain can shout the words quickly or slowly.

4 If someone touches the line or goes the wrong way, they're out. The last person still playing is the winner.

What's the noise?

1 Someone thinks of a noise to make. It could be:

a police   a phone   a dog   a horse   or a door
siren...   ringing...   barking...   galloping...   creaking open...

2 They make the noise to someone else, using their mouth or hands. (If you're in a car, don't make sudden noises that will distract the driver.)

To make the sound of a police siren, make a "whoo-whoo" noise with your mouth:

For a horse galloping, you could clap your hands to make the sound of pounding hooves:

3 The other person tries to guess what the noise is.

Hmmm...
Is it a heart
beating..?

4 If they are correct, they make the next noise. If not, they can continue guessing. If they decide to give up guessing, the first person can make another noise.

37

Lots of legs

Two people can play this game in a car, train or bus.

1 Each person looks out of a different side.
Someone starts the game by saying Lots of legs! and both people try to spot legs, such as:

a person's legs...   the legs on a chair or table...   an animal's legs...   or legs on a sign...

2 Each time someone spots some legs, they call out:

Cow! Four legs!

Four legs on that bench!

A jogger! Two legs!

Two chairs – eight legs!

Each person keeps a count of how many legs they see altogether.

3 The first person to spot 20 legs wins the game.

Still as a statue

1 Choose someone to be a statue. The statue can stand or sit, and has to stay completely still.

2 Everyone else tries to make the statue move. They're not allowed to touch her, but they can try:

making faces...

Why did the chicken cross the road?

telling jokes...

doing funny dances...

3 When the statue moves, smiles or laughs, it's someone else's turn to be the statue.

Tip
This game can be played in a car, but no one should shout or yell, or they'll distract the driver.

Wall ball

For this game, you need a wall to play against, and a small ball. Choose someone to be the thrower.

1 The thrower stands five paces from the wall, and everyone else stands in a line against it.

Thrower

Mark each end of the line with a sweater.

2 The thrower throws the ball at everyone else's legs, and they jump in the air to avoid it. If someone is hit below the knee, they change places with the thrower.

Stay between the sweaters.

3 Continue until everyone has been the thrower.

Treasure hunt

To play this, you'll need some paper and some pens.

1 Draw a big desert island with an X for the start and a circle for treasure.

Draw two palm trees, too.

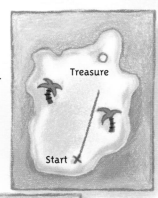

2 One person puts a pen on the X and shuts his eyes. He draws a straight line and aims for the treasure:

3 The other person draws a line in the same way. Then, whoever is furthest from the treasure draws, with their eyes shut, a line from the end of their last line.

4 Continue until both people reach the treasure. Whoever drew the fewest lines wins.

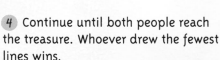

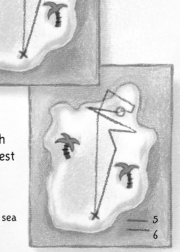

Any lines that go into the sea count as two lines.

5
6

Think of 10

1 Someone thinks of a category of things, such as:

food · animals · countries · vehicles

2 The other person has one minute to think of 10 things in that category. If they think of 10, they get one point.

> Bread... apples... chicken... carrots... chocolate...

3 Each person takes turns thinking of a category. The first person to get five points wins.

Tip
'Food' is an easy category, because there are so many kinds of food. For a harder game, choose a category with fewer things in it, such as vegetables.

Pass it on

For this game, you need a ball and something that plays music. Choose someone to be the music-maker.

1 Everyone else sits in a circle, and one person is given the ball. The music-maker starts the music.

2 The person with the ball very quickly passes it to the person next to them, and so on.

Pass the ball as quickly as you can.

3 At some point, the music-maker stops the music without warning.

4 The person holding the ball is out. They give the ball to the person next to them and leave the circle. Then, the game continues.

5 The last person still playing is the winner.

Sad face, happy face

1 In this counting game, some numbers are replaced with making sad and happy faces:

SAD FACE — Make this face instead of saying any number with 5 in it.

HAPPY FACE — Make this face instead of saying any number with 7 in it.

2 Everyone counts up from 1, taking turns saying a number or making a face:

...3   ...4   ...5   ...6   ...7   ...8

Three   Four   sad face   Six   happy face   Eight

3 Continue to take turns, and watch out for 57 and 75, because they contain both a 5 and a 7:

17	25	37	57
happy face	sad face	happy face	sad face, happy face

4 If anyone hesitates or makes a mistake, they're out.

Changing shapes

Each person playing this game needs a piece of paper and some pens or pencils.

1 Each person draws a shape, but doesn't reveal it.

Draw an outine or a filled-in shape:

2 Everyone passes their paper to someone else. They all draw on the shape they've been given, to make it into something.

This shape could be turned into:

This shape could become:

a sail or...   a silly hat   a monster or...   flames

3 Everyone shows each other what they've drawn. In the next game, everyone thinks of a different shape.

Hit the ship

Play this game on a sandy beach.

1 Draw a big ship in damp sand (see below), then add a line, six paces away. Find a pebble for each person, then stand behind the line.

2 Take turns throwing a pebble onto the ship. You get points as follows:

Top half of the ship

If a pebble lands:
On a porthole: 5
On the top half of the ship: 2
Anywhere on the ship: 1
Anywhere else: 0

Porthole

Pick up the pebble before the next person throws theirs.

Keep score in the sand:
Sam ||| Alex |||
(write five like this: ||||)

3 The first person to get 10 points wins.

Variation
If you're by yourself, keep trying to beat your score.

Dozing dogs

Play this game somewhere you can lie down safely.

1 Choose someone to be the trainer. Everyone else is a dozing dog. The dogs all lie totally still on the floor and pretend to be asleep.

2 The trainer walks around between the dogs, and tries to get them to move by making them laugh.

She can make silly noises or tell jokes...

...but she's not allowed to touch the dogs.

3 If a dog moves at all, he joins the trainer and tries to make the other dogs move.

4 The last dog still playing is the winner.

Simon says

Choose someone to be 'Simon'. Everyone else has to do what he says.

1 'Simon' tells everyone to do an action...

Simon says...
jump!

...and they all do it. Anyone who doesn't do the
action immediately is out.

2 'Simon' tells everyone to do more actions. If he doesn't start
an instruction with Simon says, everyone should ignore him...

Touch
your nose!

...and if anyone does the action, they're out.

3 The last person still playing is the winner
and becomes 'Simon' in the next game.

Mystery number

1 Someone thinks of a number between 1 and 100, and everyone else has to guess what it is.

74

2 They take turns asking questions that can be answered with Yes or No, such as:

Is it bigger than 6?

Does it have a 4 in it?

Is it smaller than 81?

Yes... Yes... Yes!

3 Continue until someone guesses the number.

Yes!

Is it 74?

4 Play again, with someone else thinking of a number.

Variations
Harder game: think of a number between 1 and 200.
Younger children: think of a number between 1 and 20.

French cricket

For this game, you'll need a tennis ball and a bat or a tennis racket. One person is the batter, and everyone else is a fielder.

1 A fielder throws the ball and tries to hit the batter below her knees. She tries to hit the ball away.

The batter protects her legs with her racket and mustn't move her feet.

2 One of these two things happens next:

The batter's leg is hit by the ball and she is out...

...or the batter hits the ball. She has to pass the racket once around her body to score a point.

Ooof!

Keep track of your points.

3 If the batter has hit the ball, the fielders chase it. If someone catches it, the batter is out. If a fielder picks up the ball, he can't move until he's thrown it at the batter. Whoever gets the batter out bats next. At the end, the person with the most points wins.

What's the word?

1 One person thinks of a word that is three to six letters long.

apple

2 The other person shuts their eyes and holds out a hand, with the palm facing up.

3 The first person uses a fingertip to slowly spell out the word on their friend's hand, one letter at a time.

Say if you're writing capital or 'little' letters.

4 The friend can try to guess the word at any time. If they're correct, they win. If not, the first person wins.

a...p...p... apple?

A to Z spotting

Play this game in a car or in a busy place. Everyone has to try to spot things that start with the letters of the alphabet. Agree which letters are too difficult (such as Q, X or Z) and leave them out.

1 Everyone tries to spot something beginning with A. The first person to do so shouts out what they've spotted...

2 ...then everyone tries to spot something beginning with B.

3 Continue through the rest of the alphabet. If a letter takes too long, agree to move onto the next one.

Quicksand

Play this game on a sandy beach or on grass.

1 First choose someone to be 'it'.

Got you!

2 Everyone runs around and 'it' tries to 'tag' (touch) them.

3 If someone is tagged, they become stuck in quicksand, and have to stand like this:

4 Someone else can free them by crawling between their legs.

Someone who is crawling can still be tagged.

5 Continue until everyone's stuck. The last person to be caught is 'it' in the next game.

53

Moon, stars, sky

In this game, everyone takes turns thinking
of a word that links up with the word before.

1 Someone
starts the game
by saying a word:

moon...

2 Someone else thinks of a word
that they associate with the first
word, then they say it out loud:

stars...

3 Then the next person
says a word that links up
with the word that's just
been said...

sky...

4 ...and everyone takes turns to add a word:

blue...   red...   strawberry...

5 If anyone repeats a word,
they're out. The game continues
until only one person is left or
someone can't think of a word.

melon...

Making boxes

In this game, two people take turns to join dots to make boxes. You'll need paper and pens or pencils.

1 Draw seven rows of seven dots on a piece of paper. One person draws a line between two dots, then the other person adds a line.

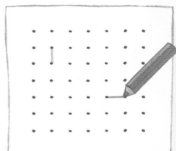

The lines must be horizontal or vertical, not diagonal.

2 Take turns adding lines. If someone makes a box when they add a line, they write their initial in the box. Then, they draw another line on the grid.

3 At the end of the game, count how many boxes each person has made. Whoever has the most boxes wins.

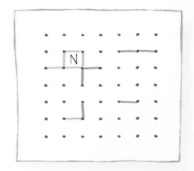

Clapping catch

For this game, you'll need a ball.
Each person has three lives.

1 Everyone stands a few paces from each other:

2 Someone throws the ball to someone else, shouting a number from 1 to 5 as they throw it. The other person has to clap that number of times before they catch it:

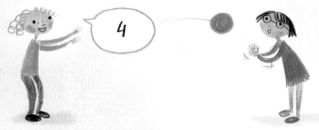

3 If they manage it, they throw the ball to the next person and shout a number. If not, they lose a life.

4 The last person still playing is the winner.

I'm going to...

1 Someone thinks of a place they might go to on a trip and the others have to guess where it is. It could be:

A beach in
Australia...

...mountains in
Switzerland...

...or somewhere
closer to home.

2 Everyone else takes turns asking questions that can only be answered with Yes or No. They can ask a total of 12 questions.

3 If someone thinks that they know what the place is, they can guess, but it counts as a question. If they are correct, they win.

4 If no one guesses the place, the person who thought of it wins.

Mixed-up answers

1 One person starts by saying a word. It can be absolutely anything...

Cookie

2 The other person replies with a question that has the word as its answer.

What might you eat as a snack?

3 The first person replies with a word that doesn't answer the question:

Dog

4 The other person has to think of a question that this new word could be the answer to.

Which pet do you take for a walk?

Um... er...

5 Continue until the second person makes a mistake or hesitates for too long. Then, change places and play again.

Robot drawing game

Everyone needs a piece of paper and a pen. If you're by yourself, use ideas from this page to draw a robot.

1 Each person draws a robot's head on their paper.

2 They pass their paper to someone else, who adds a shape for a body.

3 Everyone passes on their paper again.

4 Continue the game, adding something new each time:

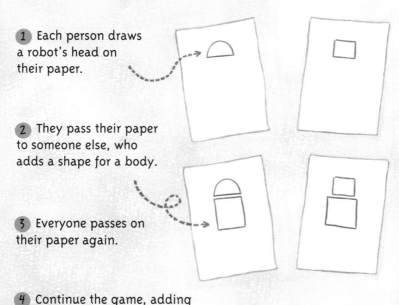

buttons   antennae   eyes

legs   arms   wheels

Hidden hands

In this game, two people try to win by showing each other one of these three hand shapes:

Scissors   Paper   Rock

1 Each person makes a shape behind their back.

2 They both count to three...

One... two... three!

One... two... three!

...then each show their hidden hand at the same time.

3 Any of the three hand shapes can win, depending on what the other person has chosen to do:

Scissors beat paper, because they cut it.

Paper beats rock, because it wraps it.

Rock beats scissors, as it blunts them.

4 Play until someone has won five games.

I've got five

Each person needs paper and a pen or a pencil.

1 Everyone agrees on five categories of things to think of. They all write them down:

animals	countries	fruit and vegetables	vehicles	boys' names

2 One person thinks of a letter of the alphabet...

...and everyone has to write down something that begins with that letter in each category.

animals	countries	fruit and vegetables	vehicles	boys' names
CAT	CHINA	CARROT	CAR	CHARLIE

3 The first person to write something in every category shouts I've got five! and everyone stops writing.
Add up everyone's scores, like this:

> Correct answer — 2 points
> Correct answer shared with someone else — 1 point
> Shouting I've got five! — 2 bonus points

4 Everyone takes turns to think of a letter.
At the end, add up the scores to see who has won.

Musical chairs

You need something that plays music and some chairs — one per person, minus one. Choose someone to be the music-maker but don't put out a chair for them.

1 Group the chairs together, then stand around them. The music-maker starts the music, and everyone else dances around the chairs.

If four people are playing, use three chairs.

2 Suddenly, the music-maker stops the music. Everyone else has to try to sit down on a chair.
The person who doesn't get a chair is out.

Only one person can sit on each chair.

3 Everyone stands up and one chair is taken away.

4 The music starts again, and the game continues until there is only one chair left. When the music stops again, whoever is sitting on the chair is the winner.

Filling a pie

This is a memory game. Everyone has to add to a list of ingredients that are going into an imaginary pie.

1 Someone says...

> When I bake a pie, I fill it with...

2 ...then they add an ingredient that isn't usually found in a pie, such as:

> ice cream...

3 The next person repeats the phrase, and adds their own ingredient:

> When I bake a pie, I fill it with ice cream... and lettuce...

4 Everyone takes turns adding ingredients, always saying them in the correct order:

> When I bake a pie, I fill it with ice cream... lettuce... chicken soup... and cookies...

5 If anyone forgets an ingredient or says the ingredients in the wrong order, they're out.

Sardines

Play this hiding game inside or outside.

1 One person is the hider, and everyone else is a seeker. The seekers cover their eyes and count to 50...

...while the hider runs off to find a place to hide.

2 When the seekers get to 50, they look for the hider. If someone finds him, they hide with him.

Each seeker who finds the hiding place hides there too.

3 Continue playing until the last seeker finds everyone else.

Story consequences

Each person needs a strip of paper and a pen.

1 Everyone starts by writing a word that could describe a man at the top of their paper...

2 ...then they fold over the paper, to hide the word.

3 Everyone passes on their paper to someone else...

...and the game continues in the same way. These are the things that everyone has to write next:

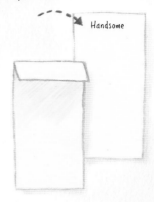

A man's name

MET... a word to describe a woman

A woman's name

AT... a place

HE SAID TO HER: a phrase

SHE SAID TO HIM: a phrase

THEN... an ending for the story

Handsome

Prince Charming

MET...beautiful

Snow White

AT... the skate park

HE SAID TO HER:
What an amazing hat!

SHE SAID TO HIM:
I'm hungry

THEN...
a blue camel plodded past

4 At the end, pass on the pieces of paper again, then unfold them and read the stories.

Snail trail

Play this game on a sandy beach. Draw a snail shell in damp sand (or on the ground with a chalk), then add short lines to make boxes.

1 Hop around the shell, one box at a time.

Land on one foot and don't land on any lines, or you'll have to start again.

Home

Start here.

2 Jump onto 'Home' in the middle. Then, turn around and hop back to the start.

Land on both feet.

3 If you reach the start without landing on any lines, write your initial in one of the boxes.

Jump onto this box next time.

4 Hop around again, but jump onto the marked box with both feet. Continue hopping, jumping and writing your initials until you've filled all the boxes.

I don't spy

This game is the opposite of 'I spy'.
It's a chance for people to use their imagination.

1. One person thinks of
something that they can't see
anywhere, such as a penguin.

2. They say, I don't spy with
my little eye..., then give two
clues: the kind of thing it is
(bird) and its first letter (P).

I don't spy with my little eye...

Pelican?

3. Everyone
else takes turns
guessing what
the first person is
thinking of.

Pigeon?

4. The first person to guess correctly thinks of
another object and the game starts again.

Ping bong

For this game, you need a ball, and someone to be the thrower. Each person has three lives. The noise PING means catch, and BONG means drop.

1 Everyone stands apart from each other, like this:

Thrower

2 The thrower throws the ball to someone, shouting PING or BONG at the same time.

PING!

Catch the ball

BONG!

Drop the ball

The catcher has to do what the noise means. If they get it wrong, they lose one of their three lives.

3 Return the ball back to thrower, and the game continues with the thrower throwing to people at random, until only one other person is left.

Grid game

To play this game, you'll need paper, and pens or pencils. First decide who draws O and who draws X.

1 Then, draw a grid on the paper:

2 One person draws an O in one of the squares...

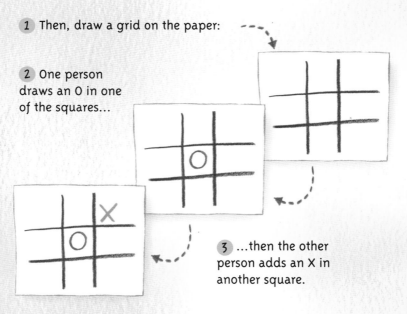

3 ...then the other person adds an X in another square.

4 Take turns adding Os and Xs. The first to make a line of three is the winner:

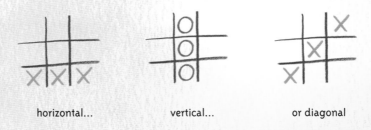

horizontal...   vertical...   or diagonal

If no one manages to make a line of three shapes, no one has won and the game is a draw.

Guess the letter

1 Someone thinks of a letter in the alphabet for everyone else to try to guess.

2 Everyone else takes turns asking questions that can be answered Yes or No. They can ask a total of 10 questions between them, such as:

Is it in the word 'queen'?

Is it before F?

Yes... No.

3 If someone thinks they know which letter it is, they can guess, as one of the 10 questions. If they're correct, they win. If not, they're out.

Is it Q?

Yes!

4 If no one guesses the letter, the person who thought of it has won.

Mr. Wolf

1 Choose someone to be Mr. Wolf. He stands with his back to everyone else, twelve paces away from them.

Everyone else asks Mr. Wolf the time:

Mr. Wolf doesn't turn around. He answers by saying a time:

> What's the time, Mr. Wolf?

> Four o'clock

2 As Mr. Wolf has said Four o'clock, everyone takes four steps forward, counting the steps out loud:

> One, two, three, four...

3 They stop and ask the time again. At any point, Mr. Wolf can turn around and shout Dinner time! instead of saying a time. He then chases everyone until he catches someone, who becomes the next Mr. Wolf.

> Dinner time!

4 If someone manages to reach Mr. Wolf and touch him before he shouts Dinner time!, everyone is safe and Mr. Wolf has to be Mr. Wolf again in the next game.

Copy me

To play this game, everyone has to face each other.

1 Someone starts by doing an action, such as:

Patting their stomach...

2 The next person repeats the action, then adds a new action of their own:

They pat their stomach...   ...then scrunch their nose.

3 Everyone takes turns adding an action, always doing all the actions in the correct order.

Stomach pat   Nose scrunch   Hand clap

4 Anyone who forgets an action or does the actions in the wrong order is out.

Stop, thief...

For this game, you need some coins or spoons in a sock, a chair and a scarf. Choose a guard and tie the scarf around their eyes. Then, place the sock under the chair.

1 The guard sits on the chair and everyone else stands in a line a little way away.

2 Someone tiptoes up to the chair, and tries to take the sock and return to the line without being heard.

3 If the guard thinks he hears a sound, he shouts Stop! and points to where he thinks the person is.

Stop!

4 If he's correct, that person is out. If not, the sock is put back and someone else tries to take it.

5 Take turns to try to take the sock. The last person still playing wins and is the next guard.

Follow-on words

1 Someone starts by saying a word. It doesn't matter how long or short it is:

2 The next person has to say a word that starts with the last letter of the first word.

3 Take turns adding a new word.

4 Play until someone can't think of a word, or everyone agrees that they want to stop.

Shape drawings

For this drawing game, you'll need some paper and pens or pencils.

1 Someone chooses a shape, such as:

circle   triangle   square   egg   diamond   oval   rectangle

2 Someone else thinks of a subject for everyone to draw. It can be absolutely anything, such as:

a house   a dog   a car   a fish

3 Everyone draws the subject, using only the shape that's been chosen:

You could fill in the drawings with pens or pencils.

A house drawn using diamonds   A dog drawn using squares   A car drawn using ovals   A fish drawn using triangles

Land, sea, air

To play this game, draw a line in the sand on a beach or on the ground with a chalk. One side of the line is the land and the other side is the sea.

1 Choose a commander, then stand with one foot on either side of the line. The commander stands at the end of the line and shouts instructions, as follows:

If the commander shouts Land! or Sea!, everyone has to jump to that side of the line.

If she shouts Air! everyone has to jump straight up in the air, wherever they are.

2 Anyone who touches the line or makes a mistake is out. The last person still playing is the winner.

Moo... Baa!

To play this game, make a circle facing each other.

1 Each person chooses an animal noise, then makes the noise, so that the others can hear how it sounds:

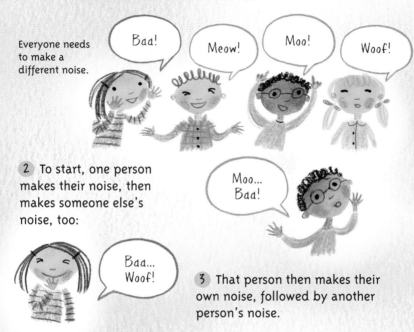

Everyone needs to make a different noise.

Baa!

Meow!

Moo!

Woof!

2 To start, one person makes their noise, then makes someone else's noise, too:

Moo... Baa!

Baa... Woof!

3 That person then makes their own noise, followed by another person's noise.

4 The game continues with each player making their own noise, followed by someone else's:

Woof... Meow!

Meow... Baa!

Baa... Moo!

Moo... Baa!

You can make the noise of the person who just chose you.

5 If anyone makes the wrong noise, or makes the noises in the wrong order, they are out.

Question catch

For this game, you need a ball. Everyone spreads out to play the game, and each person has three lives.

1 One person thinks of a simple question to ask someone else:

What's a baby sheep called?

2 They say someone's name at random, then ask them the question and throw the ball to them.

Rosie...
What's a baby sheep called?

3 The named person has to answer the question before or as they catch the ball. They lose a life if they answer wrongly or too late, or if they fail to catch the ball.

A lamb!
Oh no, I've dropped the ball!

4 Continue to throw the ball from person to person and ask questions. The last person with any lives wins.

What's my job?

1 Someone thinks of a job, but doesn't say what it is. It could be:

a nurse...

a chef...

an artist...

2 Everyone else tries to guess the job, taking turns asking questions that can be answered Yes or No. They can ask a total of 10 questions.

Do you work in an office?

Do you wear a uniform?

3 If someone thinks they know what the job is, they can guess. If they are correct, they win. If not, the guess counts as one of the 10 questions.

4 If no one guesses the job, the person who thought of it wins. Then, play again.

I'm an author!

79

Spotting rhymes

1 Someone spots something, and says what it is. It could be:

a tree...   a cat...   a house...   a cow...

2 Someone else thinks of a word that rhymes with the first word...

tree...
...bee!

It doesn't have to be something that you can see.

3 ...and the next person thinks of another word that rhymes with it:

me!

4 Everyone takes turns thinking of rhyming words, until someone can't think of one.

key

knee

tea

yippee!

5 For the next game, someone else spots something.

Party game

In this game, everyone takes turns thinking of things they'd bring to an imaginary party, such as:

balloons   cupcakes   plates   party hats   drinks

1 Someone starts the game by saying:

Amy

For our party, I'm going to bring... cupcakes.

2 Someone else then says what the first person is bringing, and adds something new:

For our party, Amy's bringing cupcakes and I'm going to bring plates.

Ben

3 The next person adds something else...

Jessica

For our party, Amy's bringing cupcakes, Ben's bringing plates, and I'm going to bring balloons.

4 ...and the game continues with each person repeating the list and adding something new.

5 If someone forgets something, or says the wrong thing, they're out. The last person still playing wins.

Winking killer

1 Play this game with as many people as possible. One person is a winking killer, and someone else is a detective. The killer winks at people to 'kill' them, but if the detective spots the killer winking at someone, the game is over.

2 One person is chosen to be the detective, then he leaves the room. Everyone else chooses someone to be the killer. The detective comes back in and everyone stands in a circle. Then the game begins:

The killer winks at someone, and they fall to the ground...

She winks at more people, one at a time. The detective has to identify her before she kills everyone.

Detective

If the detective manages to identify the killer, the killer is the next detective. If he doesn't identify her, he is the detective again.

It's YOU!

Funny animals

Each person needs paper, and a pen or pencil.

1 Fold each piece of paper in half, then unfold it again:

2 Draw the top half of an animal on the top half of the paper. Draw lines going over the fold a little, too.

3 Fold back the top half of the paper to hide the drawing. Then, pass the paper to someone else.

The lines that overlap the fold will still show.

4 Draw the bottom half of an animal, then unfold each piece of paper to reveal an animal.

83

Magician's spell

Draw a circle on the ground with a chalk, or in sand on a beach. Agree the boundaries of the playing area, then choose someone to be the magician.

1 The magician stands still inside the circle and everyone else walks around it.

2 Suddenly, the magician jumps in the air and shouts:

Pow... Zap... Abracadabra!

3 The magician runs out of the circle and tries to 'tag' (touch) everyone. When someone is tagged, they have to freeze and stay in that position.

4 Continue playing until everyone has been tagged. Whoever was tagged first becomes the next magician.

Build a ship

For this guessing game, you'll need paper and a pen.

1 One person thinks of a word and draws a short line for each letter on the paper, like this:

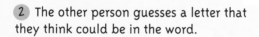

2 The other person guesses a letter that they think could be in the word.

If the letter is in the word, the first person writes it in the correct place...

...but if it isn't, he draws the first part of a ship and writes the letter to the side, like this:

3 The game continues with the first person filling in letters or adding to the ship, in the following stages:

4 The second person can try to guess the word at any time. If they're correct, they win. If they're wrong, another part is added to the ship. The first person wins if they finish drawing the whole ship.

Dodge the ball

To play this game, you'll need a soft ball, and lots of space. Agree the boundaries of your playing area, and choose someone to be the thrower.

1 The thrower stands still in the middle of the playing area and everyone else runs around.

Thrower

2 The thrower throws the ball at everyone else's legs. If someone is hit below the knee, they're out.

3 The thrower collects the ball and continues throwing until everyone's out. The last person to be out is the thrower in the next game.

Who am I?

1 To start, someone thinks of a person or a character that everyone knows, for the others to guess...

Sleeping Beauty

2 They give a clue about the person, and everyone else has one guess each:

I'm in a fairytale – who am I?

Are you... Snow White?

Are you... Bluebeard?

3 If someone is correct, they think of a new person for the others to guess. If no one guesses correctly, they are given another clue:

I'm asleep!

You must be Sleeping Beauty!

4 Continue playing until someone guesses who the person is, then play again.

Talking scraps

For this game, you'll each need scraps of paper and a pen or pencil.

1 Each person writes a subject to talk about on a scrap of paper, then folds it twice. Someone mixes all the scraps together.

food

animals

pizza

hairy spiders

2 Someone takes a scrap and unfolds it. They have to talk about the subject on it for 30 seconds. They must not say um, leave long pauses, or repeat anything.

There are so many animals in the world: big elephants, little tiny ants, um...

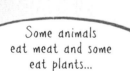

Some animals eat meat and some eat plants...

3 If someone notices a mistake, they challenge the talker. They take over from the talker and talk about the subject for the remaining time.

4 Whoever is talking at the end of 30 seconds gets one point. Everyone takes turns until all the scraps have been used. Whoever has the most points wins.

Running statue

Play this game in a big space. Choose someone to be a statue.

1 One person stands in the middle of the space, and the statue runs around her until she shouts:

Statue!

2 He instantly freezes where he is, like a statue.

3 The other person tries to make him move. She can't touch him, but can tell jokes, make noises or sing.

4 When the statue moves, play again, with the other person taking a turn at being the statue.

Animal circles

To play this game, each person needs a piece of paper and some pencils or pens.

1 Everyone draws a large circle for a body and fills it in. They add a circle for the head...

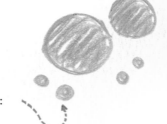

2 ...and four small circles for feet:

3 Everyone passes their paper to someone else, then they all use a pen to make the circles into animals:

Add pointed ears, a tail and whiskers for a cat.

You could draw two feet so the circles become a bird.

For a tall giraffe, draw the head and feet a long way from the body.

Walk like a robot

Play this game in a big space.

1 Everyone thinks of something that they're going to walk like. They don't tell the others what it is:

Robot   Ballerina   Penguin   Sleepwalker

2 Then, everyone walks around in the style of whatever they've thought of.

3 Everyone tries to guess what the others are walking like.

Are you a waiter?

You're a penguin!

4 If someone's walk is guessed correctly, they are out, and stop walking around. People can only guess while they are playing. The winner is the last person walking.

Down on one knee!

For this game, you need a ball. Stand a little way apart and take turns throwing the ball to each other.
If anyone fails to catch the ball, this happens:

The first time, everyone else shouts:

Down on one knee!

...and the person has to continue playing with one knee on the ground.

The second time someone drops the ball, they put one hand behind their back, too.

The third time they drop it, they have to close one eye as well.

If someone drops the ball a fourth time, they're out.
The last person still playing is the winner.

Eat the alphabet

In this game, everyone adds to a list of foods in the order of the alphabet. Agree which letters are too hard (such as Q, X or Z) and leave them out.

1 Someone says that they're going to eat a kind of food that starts with an A:

I'm HUNGRY! I'm going to eat an apricot.

I'm HUNGRY! I'm going to eat a banana.

2 The next person repeats the first part of the sentence, then adds a food beginning with B.

3 Someone else adds a food beginning with C, and the game continues with everyone taking turns:

...cheese...

...a date...

...an egg...

...fruit...

4 If anyone can't think of a food that begins with the next letter, they're out.

Touch tag

For this game, you'll need a big space and lots of people. Agree the boundaries of the playing area, and choose someone to be 'it'. Then, play the game:

Everyone runs around, and 'it' has to try to 'tag' (touch) them...

'It'

IT!

...If she tags someone, she shouts IT! and that person becomes 'it' instead.

No returns!

The new 'it' has to give the old 'it' a chance to run away from him. If he tries to tag her immediately, the old 'it' shouts...

...She then has a chance to run away, and the game continues.

Play until everyone has been 'it', or everyone agrees that they want to stop playing.

Mixed-up faces

For this drawing game, each person needs a piece of paper and some pens or pencils.

1 Someone thinks of a kind of person, such as:

a princess...   a pirate...   a singer...   or a king...

2 Everyone draws a shape for that kind of person's head.

A princess's head...

...with a singer's hair.

3 Someone else says another kind of person. Everyone adds that kind of hair to their drawings:

4 The game continues in the same way, like this:

a nose   ears   eyes   a mouth

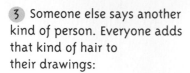

an old man   a fairy   a pirate   a baby

5 Then, everyone shows their drawings to each other.

Artist at work

For this drawing game, you'll need paper, and a pen or pencil.
Choose someone to be the 'artist'.

1 The artist thinks of something to draw that won't be too easy for the others to guess.

2 The artist starts to draw the object, a shape at a time.

Start with a shape that could be part of something else:

Add more shapes, one at a time:

3 Everyone else tries to guess what they're drawing.

What could this be?   a robot...   a house on a hill...   or...

 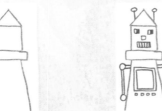 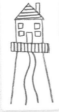 

4 The artist continues until someone guesses what they are drawing. The first to guess correctly is the next artist.

It's a lighthouse!

Stop the story

In this game, everyone tries to stop a story from being told. They take turns adding a word, and try to make it impossible for the next person to add one.

1 Someone starts by saying a word...

Thick...

...fog...

2 ...then someone else adds another one:

3 The game continues in the same way, until someone is stuck and can't add a word:

...made...   ...it...   ...impossible...   ...to...   ...see...

Tip
If someone says a word that is hard to follow, words such as but or and can help to continue the story.

...but...

97

Beach target game

Play this game on a sandy beach.

1 Draw a line in damp sand with a stick, then find a pebble for each person.

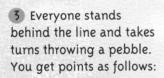

2 Draw a small circle six paces from the line. Then, add three larger circles around it.

3 Everyone stands behind the line and takes turns throwing a pebble. You get points as follows:

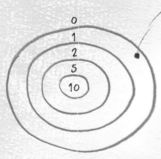

0
1
2
5
10

Keep score in the sand:
Anya ||| Fred ||||
(write five like this: ||||)

4 The first to 20 points wins.

Variation
If you're by yourself, keep trying to beat your highest score.

Race to base

Play this game in a big space. Agree the boundaries of the playing area, then draw a chalk line down the middle. Draw a base at each end, then form two teams. Each team has to guard their base.

1 Someone shouts Go! and the game begins:

Each person tries to get to the other team's base...

Red half   Blue half

Red base   Blue base

If someone manages to get there, they win a point for their team. Both teams go back to their own half and the game starts again...

While someone is in the other team's half, someone from that team can tag them and they have to freeze...

...until someone from their own team tags them again and sets them free.

2 Keep score as you play, and continue until one team has five points, or everyone agrees to stop playing.

Big fat spiders

1 Someone starts by asking a simple question, such as:

> What do you like to eat for lunch?

2 Someone else replies:

> Big fat spiders!

Try not to laugh, because anyone who laughs is out.

3 Someone else asks a question...

> What do you brush your hair with?

4 ...and the next person replies:

> Big fat spiders!

Everyone has to keep trying not to laugh.

5 Everyone takes turns to ask more questions. Each time, someone else has to answer Big fat spiders!
The last person to laugh is the winner.

> What's on my head?

> Big fat spiders!

> What do you fill pies with?

> Big fat spiders!

Fierce Mr. Crocodile

Use chalk to draw two lines on the ground for a river. Then, choose someone to be Mr. Crocodile.

1 Mr. Crocodile stands in the river. The others all stand on one side of the river and ask:

> Fierce Mr. Crocodile, may we cross your river?

Mr. Crocodile

River

2 Mr. Crocodile replies: Only if you're wearing something..., then says something such as ...red!

Anyone who's wearing what he said can walk across the river safely...

...but everyone else has to run across without being 'tagged' (touched) by Mr. Crocodile.

3 Anyone who is tagged is out. The game continues in the same way, with Mr. Crocodile giving a different answer each time. The last person to be tagged wins and is the next Mr. Crocodile.

Bouncing ball

To play this game, you'll need a ball.

1 One person starts by bouncing the ball once to someone else and they have to catch it.

You can bounce the ball softly or hard, high or low.

2 Take turns bouncing the ball to each other.

3 If someone misses or drops the ball, they get a penalty point.

Low bounces are hard to catch.

4 Each time anyone misses or drops the ball, they get another penalty point.

5 When someone has five penalty points, they are out of the game.

6 The last person still playing is the winner.

What's my hobby?

1 One person thinks of a hobby (real or imagined) and the others have to find out what it is.

It could be rollerskating...

dancing...

...or drawing.

playing a guitar...

Do you do this hobby outside?

Yes

2 They can ask her a total of 10 questions that can be answered with just Yes or No.

3 If someone thinks they know the hobby, they can guess, but the guess counts as a question. If they're correct, they win.

4 If no one guesses the hobby, the person who thought of it wins.

It's surfing!

Animals in the zoo

1 Someone starts the game by saying:

I went to the zoo and I saw a tiger...

2 The next person has to think of an animal that starts with the last letter of the animal that's been said.

TIGER... RHINO!

3 They repeat the sentence, adding their animal.

I went to the zoo and I saw a rhino...

I went to the zoo and I saw an ostrich...

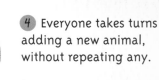

4 Everyone takes turns adding a new animal, without repeating any.

5 The game continues until someone can't think of an animal that follows on from the last one.

Picture consequences

1 Each person needs a strip of paper and a pen or a pencil. Start by drawing a head and neck at the top of the paper...

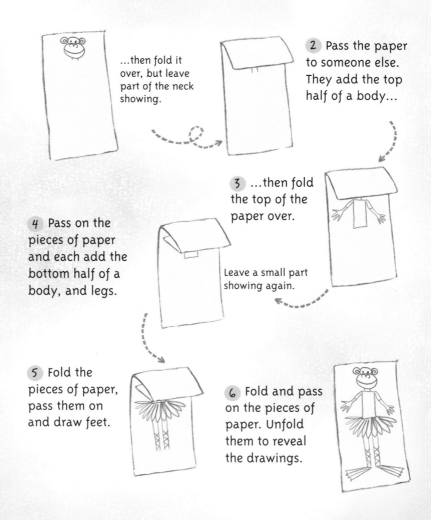

...then fold it over, but leave part of the neck showing.

2 Pass the paper to someone else. They add the top half of a body...

3 ...then fold the top of the paper over.

Leave a small part showing again.

4 Pass on the pieces of paper and each add the bottom half of a body, and legs.

5 Fold the pieces of paper, pass them on and draw feet.

6 Fold and pass on the pieces of paper. Unfold them to reveal the drawings.

Treasure chase

Play this game on a sandy beach. Draw two big shapes for islands and form two teams. Put three objects for 'treasure' on each island for the teams to guard.

1 Each team has to try to steal a piece of the other team's treasure and bring it back to their own island.

Someone runs onto the other island to steal a piece of the treasure...

...but if someone on the other team tags (touches) them, they are stuck...

...until someone from their own team frees them.

2 Continue playing until one team gets all three pieces of the other team's treasure back to their island.

Story-telling game

In this imagination game, everyone adds to a story, five words at a time.

1 Someone starts by making up the first five words of the story.

Suddenly, the door creaked open...

2 Someone else adds another five words.

Or...

...and a tiny fluffy kitten...

...and the candle blew out...

3 Everyone takes turns to add five words.

...tiptoed softly in, followed by...

...as a dashing knight entered...

4 Make sure that the story makes sense.

...a princess wearing dazzling jewels...

...with his sword drawn and...

5 When everyone wants to stop playing, someone has to think of a good way to end the story.

Index